KEEP KEEP KEEP KEE
ALM CALM
FOR CALM
DS DADS

D1626578

KEEP KE
CALM CALM CALM CAL
FOR FOR FOR FOR
DADS DADS DADS DAD

EEP KEEP KEEP KEEP
ALM CALM CALM CALM
FOR FOR FOR FOR
DS DADS DADS DADS

KEEP KEEP KEEP KE
CALM CALM CALM CA
FOR FOR FOR FO
DADS DADS DADS DAD

EEP KEEP KEEP KEEP
ALM CALM CALM CALM
FOR FOR FOR FOR
DS DADS DADS DADS

KEEP CALM FOR DADS   KEEP CALM FOR DADS   KEEP CALM FOR DADS   KEEP CALM FOR DADS

KEEP CALM FOR DADS   KEEP CALM FOR DADS   KEEP CALM FOR DADS   KEEP CALM FOR DADS

KEEP CALM FOR DADS   KEEP CALM FOR DADS   KEEP CALM FOR DADS   KEEP CALM FOR DADS

KEEP CALM FOR DADS   KEEP CALM FOR DADS   KEEP CALM FOR DADS   KEEP CALM FOR DADS

KEEP CALM FOR DADS   KEEP CALM FOR DADS   KEEP CALM FOR DADS   KEEP CALM FOR DADS

KEEP

CALM

FOR

DADS

KEEP CALM FOR DADS

Summersdale Publishers Ltd
46 West Street
Chichester
West Sussex
PO19 1RP
UK

www.summersdale.com

Printed and bound in the Czech Republic

ISBN: 978-1-84953-254-9

Substantial discounts on bulk quantities of Summersdale books are available to corporations, professional associations and other organisations. For details telephone Summersdale Publishers on (+44-1243-771107), fax (+44-1243-786300) or email (nicky@summersdale.com).

KEEP
CALM
FOR
DADS

summersdale

There's no pillow quite
so soft as a father's
strong shoulder.

Richard L. Evans

Life doesn't come with an
instruction book; that's
why we have fathers.

H. Jackson Brown Jr

A good father is one of the
most unsung, unpraised,
unnoticed, and yet one
of the most valuable
assets in our society.

Billy Graham

When my kids
become wild and
unruly, I use a nice,
safe playpen. When
they're finished,
I climb out.

Erma Bombeck

It is amazing how quickly
the kids learn to drive
a car, yet are unable to
understand the lawnmower
or vacuum cleaner.

Ben Bergor

Home is a place you
grow up wanting to
leave, and grow old
wanting to get back to.

John Ed Pearce

There are times when parenthood seems nothing but feeding the mouth that bites you.

Peter De Vries

The secret of dealing
successfully with
a child is not to
be its parent.

Mell Lazarus

Being a dad is
more important
than football.

David Beckham

Children are natural mimics
who act like their parents
despite every effort to teach
them good manners.

Anonymous

Cleaning your house while
your kids are still growing is
like shovelling the sidewalk
before it stops snowing.

Phyllis Diller

Children need love,
especially when they
don't deserve it.

Harold S. Hulbert

We've had bad
luck with our kids –
they've all grown up.

Christopher Morley

Sing out loud in the car
even, or especially, if it
embarrasses your children.

Marilyn Penland

… the father is a giant
from whose shoulders
you can see for ever.

Perry Garfinkel

When you can't do anything
else to a boy, you can
make him wash his face.

Ed Howe

Parenthood is a lot easier to get into than out of.

Bruce Lansky

The toughest job in the
world isn't being a president.
It's being a parent.

Bill Clinton

A father and his car
keys are soon parted.

Anonymous

The sooner you treat your son as a man, the sooner he will be one.

John Dryden

By the time a man realises
that maybe his father was
right, he usually has a son
who thinks he's wrong.

Charles Wadsworth

Dad... a son's
first hero.

Anonymous

Being a great father is like shaving. No matter how good you shaved today, you have to do it again tomorrow.

Reed Markham

Always kiss your
children goodnight
– even if they're
already asleep.

H. Jackson Brown Jr

Dads are stone skimmers, mud wallowers, water wallopers, ceiling swoopers, shoulder gallopers, upsy-downsy, over-and-through, round-and-about whoosers.

Helen Thomson

My daddy, he was somewhere between God and John Wayne.

Hank Williams Jr

Being a father
helps me be more
responsible… you
see more things than
you've ever seen.

Kid Rock

A man's children and his
garden both reflect the
amount of weeding done
during the growing season.

Anonymous

Your children need
your presence more
than your presents.

Jesse Jackson

Setting a good example
for your children takes all
the fun out of middle age.

William Feather

My father only hit
me once – but he
used a Volvo.

Bob Monkhouse

Fatherhood is pretending
the present you love most
is soap-on-a-rope.

Bill Cosby

It is a wise father that knows his own child.

William Shakespeare

You don't raise heroes; you raise sons. And if you treat them like sons, they'll turn out to be heroes, even if it's just in your own eyes.

Walter M. Schirra Sr

Having one child makes
you a parent; having
two you are a referee.

David Frost

A child can ask
questions that a wise
man cannot answer.

Anonymous

I have found the best way
to give advice to your
children is to find out
what they want and then
advise them to do it.

Harry S. Truman

A father is a banker
provided by nature.

French proverb

To bring up a child in
the way he should go,
travel that way yourself
once in a while.

Josh Billings

I'm a father; that's
what matters most.

Gordon Brown

Fatherly love
is the ability to
expect the best
from your children
despite the facts.

Jasmine Birtles,
A Father's Little Instruction Book

It is admirable for a man
to take his son fishing,
but there is a special
place in heaven for the
father who takes his
daughter shopping.

John Sinor

There are three stages of
a man's life: he believes
in Santa Claus, he doesn't
believe in Santa Claus,
he is Santa Claus.

Anonymous

A father's solemn duty
is to watch football
with his children and
teach them when to
shout at the ref.

Paul Collins

Telling a teenager
the facts of life is like
giving a fish a bath.

Arnold H. Glasow

I looked up to my dad. He was always on a ladder.

David Chartrand

Dads regard themselves
as giant shock absorbers,
there to protect the family
from the ruts and bumps
on the road of life.

W. Bruce Cameron

A father is a guy who
has snapshots in
his wallet where his
money used to be.

Anonymous

All babies are supposed to look like me – at both ends.

Winston Churchill

There's a time for being a
rock star… but you've got
to put time aside for being
daddy, and getting chocolate
rubbed in your face.

Noel Gallagher

Never raise your hand
to your kids. It leaves
your groin unprotected.

Red Buttons

My father had a
profound influence on
me – he was a lunatic.

Spike Milligan

Blessed indeed is
the man who hears
many gentle voices
call him father!

Lydia M. Child

To be a successful father…
there's one absolute
rule: when you have a
kid, don't look at it for
the first two years.

Ernest Hemingway

It is a great moment
in life when a father
sees a son grow
taller than he.

Richard L. Evans

What we become depends on what our fathers teach us at odd moments, when they aren't trying to teach us.

Umberto Eco

Certain is it that there is
no kind of affection so
purely angelic as of a
father to a daughter.

Joseph Addison

A truly rich man is one
whose children run
into his arms when
his hands are empty.

Anonymous

I am not ashamed to say
that no man I ever met
was my father's equal.

Hedy Lamarr

To her the name of
father was another
name for love.

Fanny Fern

Safe, for a child, is
his father's hand,
holding him tight.

Marion C. Garretty

Any kid will run any
errand for you if you
ask at bedtime.

Red Skelton

What's the most
special thing about
being a father?
Everything.

Viggo Mortensen

Oh, what a tangled web
we weave when first we
practice to conceive.

Don Herold

Children are nature's
very own form of
birth control.

Dave Barry

A father is someone you
look up to, no matter
how tall you are.

Anonymous

The happiest
moments of my life
have been the few
which I have passed
at home in the bosom
of my family.

Thomas Jefferson

My dad always used to tell me that if they challenge you to an after-school fight, tell them you won't wait – you can kick their ass right now.

Cameron Diaz

It is much easier
to become a father
than to be one.

Kent Nerburn

Families with babies and
families without babies
are sorry for each other.

Ed Howe

Even when freshly
washed and relieved of
all obvious confections,
children tend to be sticky.

Fran Lebowitz

Parents are not
interested in justice
– they want QUIET!

Bill Cosby

Babies are always more
trouble than you thought
– and more wonderful.

Charles Osgood

A baby is an
inestimable blessing
and bother.

Mark Twain

Anyone who thinks the art of
conversation is dead ought
to tell a child to go to bed.

Robert Gallagher

Try to get one that
doesn't spit up.
Other than that,
you're on your own.

Calvin Trillin, *Family Man*

When you're a father, you know exactly where your heart really is. There's no question of it, no doubt.

Fred Ward

Children really
brighten up a
household. They
never turn the
lights off.

Ralph 'Bus' Wycherley

The trouble with
learning to parent on
the job is that your
child is the teacher.

Robert Brault

When I was a boy of fourteen, my father was so ignorant I could hardly stand to have the old man around. But when I got to be twenty-one, I was astonished at how much he had learned in seven years.

Mark Twain

My father was my teacher. But most importantly he was a great dad.

Beau Bridges

Everybody knows how to
raise children, except the
people who have them.

P. J. O'Rourke

A two-year-old is kind of
like having a blender, but
you don't have a top for it.

Jerry Seinfeld

A child, like your stomach, doesn't need all you can afford to give it.

Frank A. Clark

Parenthood remains
the greatest
single preserve
of the amateur.

Alvin Toffler

You can learn many
things from children.
How much patience you
have, for instance.

Franklin P. Jones

Dad taught me everything I know. Unfortunately, he didn't teach me everything he knows.

Al Unser Jr

A child enters your home…
makes so much noise you
can hardly stand it. The
child departs, leaving the
house so silent you think
you are going mad.

John Andrew Holmes

For many people,
God is just dad
with a mask on.

Anonymous

Having children makes
you no more a parent
than having a piano
makes you a pianist.

Michael Levine

It would seem that something which means poverty, disorder and violence every single day should be avoided entirely, but the desire to beget children is a natural urge.

Phyllis Diller

The trouble with
being a parent is that
by the time you are
experienced, you
are unemployed.

Anonymous

Money isn't everything
but it sure keeps
you in touch with
your children.

Jean Paul Getty

All children alarm their parents, if only because you are forever expecting to encounter yourself.

Gore Vidal

Setting too good
an example is a
kind of slander
seldom forgiven.

Benjamin Franklin

I make it a rule to pat
all children on the head
as they pass by – in
case it is one of mine.

Augustus John

You know, fathers just
have a way of putting
everything together.

Erika Cosby

The trouble with
children is that they
are not returnable.

Quentin Crisp

The secret of
fatherhood is to know
when to stop tickling.

Anonymous

Up until I became a
father, it was all about
self-obsession. But then
I learned exactly what
it's all about: the delight
of being a servant.

Eric Clapton

The most important
thing a father can do
for his children is to
love their mother.

Henry Ward Beecher

Being a father is like doing drugs – you smell bad, get no sleep and spend all your money on them.

Paul Bettany

A father is a man who
expects his children
to be as good as
he meant to be.

Carolyn Coats

Watching your daughter being collected by her date feels like handing over a million-dollar Stradivarius to a gorilla.

Jim Bishop

Youth is a wonderful thing. What a crime to waste it on children.

George Bernard Shaw

The quickest way for a
parent to get a child's
attention is to sit down
and look comfortable.

Lane Olinghouse

You have a lifetime
to work, but children
are only young once.

Polish proverb

My kids hate me. Every Father's Day they give a 'World's Greatest Dad' mug to the milkman.

Rodney Dangerfield

Each day of our lives
we make deposits into
the memory banks
of our children.

Charles R. Swindoll

If you want to
recapture your
youth, just cut off
his allowance.

Al Bernstein

Many a man wishes he were strong enough to tear a telephone book in half – especially if he has a teenage daughter.

Guy Lombardo

A lot of parents pack
up their troubles
and send them off
to summer camp.

Raymond Duncan

My father was
very important to
me, because he
made me think.

Janis Joplin

A rose can say 'I love you',
   Orchids can enthral,
   But a weed bouquet
      in a chubby fist,
   Yes, that says it all.

Anonymous

Children aren't happy
with nothing to ignore,
and that's what parents
were created for.

Ogden Nash

The problem with
children is that you
have to put up with
their parents.

Charles de Lint

Mother Nature is wonderful.
Children get too old for
piggy-back rides just
about the same time they
get too heavy for them.

Anonymous

Human beings are
the only creatures
on earth that allow
their children to
come back home.

Bill Cosby

Never underestimate
a child's ability to get
into more trouble.

Martin Mull

What's a good investment?
Go home from work
early and spend the
afternoon throwing a ball
around with your son.

Ben Stein

Happiness is having a
large, loving, caring,
close-knit family
in another city.

George Burns

Children are a great comfort
in your old age – and they
help you reach it faster, too.

Lionel Kauffman

Did you know babies are nauseated by the smell of a clean shirt?

Jeff Foxworthy

My father gave me the
greatest gift anyone could
give another person,
he believed in me.

Jim Valvano

Before I got married
I had six theories
about bringing up
children; now I
have six children,
and no theories.

John Wilmot

When I was a kid, I
used to imagine animals
running under my bed.
I told my dad... He cut
the legs off the bed.

Lou Brock

Families are like
fudge – mostly sweet
with a few nuts.

Anonymous

What do I
owe my father?
Everything.

Henry van Dyke

I've made a few nice dishes in my time, but this has got to be the best one I've ever made.

Jamie Oliver talking about his first child

BOY, n: A noise
with dirt on it.

Anonymous

There are two things
in life for which
we are never truly
prepared: twins.

Josh Billings

Here we have a baby. It
is composed of a bald
head and a pair of lungs.

Eugene Field

Children begin by
loving their parents; as
they grow older they
judge them; sometimes
they forgive them.

Oscar Wilde

Having children
gives your life a
purpose. Right now,
my purpose is to
get some sleep.

Reno Goodale

My mother taught me my ABCs. From my father I learned the glories of going to the bathroom outside.

Lewis Grizzard

The heart of a father
is the masterpiece
of nature.

Abbé Prévost

Teenagers are
God's punishment
for having sex.

Patrick Murray

Adolescence begins
when children stop asking
questions – because they
know all the answers.

Evan Esar

If your children look
up to you, you've
made a success of
life's biggest job.

Anonymous

There is a strong chance
that siblings who turn
out well were hassled
by the same parents.

Robert Brault

It is not flesh and blood
but the heart which makes
us fathers and sons.

Friedrich Schiller

One father is more
than a hundred
schoolmasters.

George Herbert

Raising kids is part joy and part guerrilla warfare.

Ed Asner

Children are
gleeful barbarians.

Joe Morgenstern

While we try to teach our
children all about life,
our children teach us
what life is all about.

Angela Schwindt

It was my father
who taught me to
value myself.

Dawn French

Parents who are afraid to put their foot down usually have children who step on their toes.

Chinese proverb

A compromise is the art of
dividing a cake in such a
way that everyone believes
he has the biggest piece.

Ludwig Erhard

The hand that rocks the cradle usually is attached to someone who isn't getting enough sleep.

John Fiebig

Fathering is not
something perfect
men do, but
something that
perfects the man.

Frank Pittman

The most extraordinary
thing about having a
child is people think I'm a
responsible human being.

Colin Farrell

Any man can be a
father but it takes
someone special
to be a dad.

Anne Geddes

KEEP
CALM
AND
DRINK
UP

KEEP CALM AND DRINK UP

£4.99

ISBN: 978 1 84953 102 3

*'In victory, you deserve champagne;
in defeat, you need it.'*

Napoleon Bonaparte

BAD ADVICE FOR GOOD PEOPLE

Keep Calm and Carry On, a World War Two government poster, struck a chord in recent difficult times when a stiff upper lip and optimistic energy were needed again. But in the long run it's a stiff drink and flowing spirits that keep us all going.

Here's a book packed with proverbs and quotations showing the wisdom to be found at the bottom of the glass.

KEEP
CALM
FOR
MUMS

KEEP CALM FOR MUMS

£4.99

ISBN: 978 1 84953 253 2

'For most exhausted mums, their idea of "working out" is a good, energetic lie-down.'

Kathy Lette

WISE WORDS FOR MOTHERS

You've got the best job in the world, apparently, but some days, when you're sleep deprived and the kids are driving you crazy, you wish you could have a day off.

No chance!

This book is packed with witty and uplifting quotations to help you get through those manic moments and keep smiling, as only a mum can.

www.summersdale.com

KEEP CALM FOR DADS

KEEP CALM FOR DADS